*To THE Sr
COUNTY ....
WOOF!*

Mary Cunningham

Diana Black

Women Only
Over Fifty

...who are still puppies at heart!

*WOOF: for the over-50 woman
itching to howl at the aging process!*

Women Only Over Fifty

Diana Black
Mary Cunningham
Melinda Richarz Bailey

Echelon Press, LLC

WOOF Acknowledgments

Acknowledgments from Diana, aka, d.d. dawg

My husband, Greg, who loves me wrinkles and all. My amazing "girls," Jennifer and Caitlin, who keep me young. Amber, Bev, Donna, Joyce, Mary Mac, Sandy, Sherry, and Wendy—WOOFers extraordinaire. Fern Boley and Lulu Lord for setting the bar so high. Carrollton Creative Writers' Club and my Sister Sojourners. And finally, Carol and Dot, the other members of the original WOOF pack—two Great Dames.

Acknowledgments from Mary, aka, Milkbone

My three grown children and granddaughter for providing great material over the years. Diana, Melinda, Carol, and Dot, and all my amazing WOOFer buddies. The Carrollton Creative Writers' Club—friends, colleagues and the Quantum Queens. Future WOOFers, The Creative Café critique group—Chris, Dee and Nita. "Old" friends in Florida and "New" friends in Georgia. Last, but not least, my husband, Ken who keeps me laughing and thinking "young."

Acknowledgments from Melinda, aka, Mad Dog

To Sid, my soul mate and friend for almost forty years. Your never-ending love and support gave me the strength to go on without you.

From d.d. dawg, Milkbone and Mad Dog

To Nathalie Moore for the great cover. To Karen Syed and Echelon Press for believing in WOOF.

Table of Contents

Introduction

ᗪOGGONE, WE'RE GOOD!
And getting better...

WOOF:

What a concept.
Women Only Over Fifty
with a "new *leash* on life."

From Oprah to Ellen to our water aerobics instructor, it's all about the *joys* of aging! How 50 is the new 30! What*ever!*

Some of us are hounded by middle-age. We're dog-tired, wrinkled as a Sharpei and barking like a bitch.

Enter: WOOF: For the over-50 woman itching to howl at the aging process.

From issues of graying hair, expanding waistlines and wrinkling tattoos, to embracing triumph over personal tragedy, WOOF raises four paws to our past accomplishments, present realizations and future dreams.

Are you up to it...dogtrotting alongside this sisterhood

taking the second half of life by the tail? We know you are. After all, the past 50 years you've gained freedom! You've gained power! You've gained wisdom!

(Don't tell us you think *weight* is the only thing you've gained. Oh, you so need WOOF...)

"A howl a day keeps the scowl away!"

d.d.dawg, Milkbone & Mad Dog

Chapter One

THE HAIR OF THE DOG

"I get a lot of cracks about my hair, mostly from men who don't have any."
—Ann Richards

Twelve *billion* hair appointments. That's what we figure. Yep, the WOOFer population is about 40 million, and we estimate each has made an average of 300 salon visits. So you'd think at some point, issues with our tresses would get easier. Yeah, right...

Well, one good thing, all that "tress stress" made choosing the first chapter a snap. The title? Normally the *hair of the dog* refers to an attempt to lessen the effects of hangovers...indulging in more of what "bit" you.

WOOFers know the more ominous meaning...

From Hair to Insanity

Example: Crazed WOOFer, poised in front of bathroom mirror, scissors in hand. Family sees the hair fly onto the bathroom sink and floor. "Time to get the hell outta Dodge!" they scream.

A study should be made of women over 50 who think

they surely can do better than the kid who actually went to school to learn the trade. "You're a hairdresser's worst nightmare!" my *hairdresser* stepdaughter remarked as she gave the cape around my neck an extra tug.

Hey! My sanity's at stake here!

I'm 90% more likely to get into arguments when having a *bad hair day*. As every WOOFer knows, "so goes my hair, so goes my day, week, month, year, etc." This theory was verified by Yale University research indicating that self-esteem and social skills suffer on days when our hair is being more uncooperative than our spouse. I don't need a Yale degree to tell me that.

The theory also applies to our canine friends. Pompy, a four-pound poodle, returned from the groomer shaved so close, he looked like a rat, except for the little pink ribbons tied on the few strands of hair that remained. He didn't make eye contact for *days*.

I can relate. I have the same reaction when some wet-behind-the-ears stylist butchers my bangs. WOOFers know what I'm talking about...that dreaded "Mamie Eisenhower look." (Note: If you're wondering, "Who the heck is Mamie Eisenhower?" *Google!*)

Milkbone

I used to want to look like Cher
And have long legs and long, black hair.
I still wouldn't mind
As time has been kind
'Cause her naval she can still bare.

Mad Dog

Salt-V-Pepper

The evening before my much-needed haircut and coloring appointment, my husband and I took an after-dinner stroll with our dog, Molly. The moment I stepped out the door, I noticed how the setting sun highlighted her graying muzzle. My thoughts went immediately to the top of my head, wondering if the sun was doing a number on my very obvious gray roots, too.

I braced for the worse when I saw my 6-foot 3-inch husband looking down at me. "Wow!" he exhaled. "You sure need to dye your hair."

Glancing at his full head of silver hair that made him look handsome and distinguished, I sheepishly commented, "Yeah. Guess I need to cover all this 'salt and pepper.'"

"Honey," he laughed. "I've got news for you. There ain't no 'pepper' left on your head!"

Milkbone

A Bone to Pick!

During meno*paws* the hair on our heads and private parts thins or disappears, while the hair on our chins gets coarse and dark!

Hair Today, Doggone Tomorrow

I slam the car door and flip open the vanity mirror.

It's true. In the light of day there's no mistaking it. My head's a Halloween pumpkin, with split ends.

Did my stylist fail Perm Wave 101? Or is she thinking that at 50, I need the "youthful" coiffure of Raggedy Ann?

"Honestly, does my hair really look *that* bad?"

Mary sits in the passenger seat with eyes glued to the dashboard. "It, uh, looks...*fine!*"

Surely my best friend wouldn't lie through her canines...I stow the ice scraper I grabbed to shave my head, start the car engine and drive off into the sunset.

Coasting to a stop in Mary's driveway, it's hard to make out what she's mumbling as she leaps from the car. I think it's, "...for the fiftieth time your hair looks...*fine!*"

Hmm, you know, maybe she's right. Sure it's a change from the dark, straight hairstyle everyone is used to seeing on me. But, change is good. Healthy even!

Swinging open my backdoor, I half-chuckle at the way

I've blown the whole thing so out of proportion.

I see my daughter. My daughter sees me. Shrieks echo off the kitchen walls like the shower scene in *Psycho*. "What in the world happened to your hair?!"

d.d.dawg

The Cutting Edge

"She's here!" I spring to the door ecstatic to see my sister after more than a year.

She squeals with a big hug, "Oh! I love your new hairstyle!"

What more can a girl—at any age—hope for than her older sister's approval?

"Guess now," she adds, "I can tell you I always *hated* your hair before."

d.d.dawg

Finding the Good in Bad Hair Days

Bad Hair Days? Not quite so devastating after seeing my 56-year-old neighbor lose her hair during chemotherapy.

After spending months hiding under various scarves and hats, the summer heat finally got to her. She announced, in no uncertain terms, "If anyone has a problem with my *lack of locks*, that's just too darn bad!" Her hair was gone, but her spirit was intact.

So the next hot, humid day, when my hair looks like the dog's after a good drenching with the garden hose, I'll think about my friend, and how she can't wait to, once again, have enough hair for a *Bad Hair Day*.

Milkbone

Do you have a "bad hair day" story?

Send your story to

GreatDames@woofersclub.com

Chapter Two

Is Chocolate Bad For Dogs?

*"My momma always said,
'Life is like a box of chocolates.'"*
—Winston Groom

Sweet mystery of life…

Dispelling the Myth

Is chocolate *really* bad for dogs?

Yes! At least for the four-legged variety. WOOFers, however, are a different breed. So, right here, right now, let's clear up any misconceptions.

Seriously, how could something so rich and luscious; something that can make most grown WOOFers lie, cheat and steal; something that can, with one delicious, melt-in-your-mouth morsel bring a meno*paw*sal, endorphin deprived, raving lunatic back from the brink of insanity; be *bad* for you?

Oh, don't pretend you don't know what we're talking about. Who hasn't searched underneath the sofa cushions in January for a stray piece of Halloween candy?

21

Speaking of Halloween, did you know that it's perfectly acceptable to buy six bags of chocolate candy and expect at least *four* bags left at the end of Trick or Treat night? Of course, you may have to turn off your lights around 7:00 pm, and hide under the bed for the rest of the evening. But, hey. It's worth a few dozen smashed eggs and a couple miles of T P.

Let's face it, WOOFers, if it weren't for chocolate, we'd all be a mean bunch of junk-yard dogs.

Milkbone

A Bone to Pick!

You finally decide to eat the chocolate you've been hiding for weeks, only to discover some dirty dog swiped it!

A Sweet Memory

My mother hated fudge. She had her reasons.

When my dad retired, he entertained himself by making chocolate fudge for all us kids and grandkids. I would hover over the warm pan, fanning and blowing to speed up the cooling process. Waiting until it completely cooled was *never* an option.

Mmm-mmm...I can almost taste that melt-in-your-mouth, heavenly goodness. Oh, yeah. Back to why my mother hated fudge.

You see, Dad liked to *vigorously* beat the butter, sugar and melted cocoa, and then raise the hand mixer in a triumphant salute. *So*...all the fudge that *didn't* make it into the pan? Mom had to clean off the kitchen floor, the kitchen cabinets, the kitchen ceiling...

Milkbone

Chocolate was so valuable in Chris Columbus' day, he lugged a bag of "New World" cocoa beans back to Spain for use as currency. Wow! Think what a typical WOOFer's pantry is worth!

Chocolate Rebellion

Every time I see my doc,
He tells me something else to stop.
I quit smoking, cut my fat,
I limit wine to just one glass.
Gave up caffeine and donuts, too.
Said adios to my fruit loops.
But then I whimpered like a pup
When he said, "Cut out chocolate!"
"Oh, Doc," I cried, "You've gone too far!
I'll never give up candy bars.
Or Rocky Road and rich fudge pie.
Don't take away my only vice!
And, Doc, have you not heard the news?
Chocolate's really good for you.
So take the pizza, ham, and booze.
I'll give up those things if *you* choose.
But fight, I will, for chocolate chips.
They sit so proudly on my hips."

Mad Dog

Ancient   civilizations   worshipped
chocolate. Imagine, centuries later
and nothing has changed.

More Chocolate, Please!

Chocolate is good for your health. According to "experts," a morsel of dark chocolate has antioxidants that are good for your body, post-meno*paw*sal or otherwise. It also helps increase metabolism. A *good* thing! Anyone who's indulged in the 70% Cacao miniature assortments knows that medicinal value is secondary. The rich taste is just an excuse to eat dinner in order to *get to dessert.*

We "Chocoholics" have long championed the role these mood-enhancing endorphins play. Unfortunately, chowing down on a five-pound box of truffles usually coincides with expanding waistlines.

But, wait. Maybe not. To the ancient Greeks, olive oil was liquid gold. Egypt's pharaohs prized almonds, but, I'm stickin' with the Aztecs who considered chocolate *sacred.* These foods share more than history, however. They're loaded with monounsaturated fatty acids (MUFA'S, pronounced *MOO*-fas), good fats that protect from chronic disease (yeah, yeah, we already know that), and according to new research, help you lose fat... ESPECIALLY AROUND YOUR MIDDLE!

Milkbone

Chocolate cookies, chocolate cake,
Chocolate brownies, rich parfait.
Chocolate pudding, smooth and creamy,
Chocolate fondue, hot and steamy.
Truffles, trifles, chocolate tortes,
Divinity and warm s'mores.
And then, of course, there's chocolate mousse,
Eclairs, fudge, and sundaes, too.
So, with this tasty list of treats,
What's a WOOFer gonna eat…
First?

Milkbone

What's your favorite chocolate story?

_____

_____

_____

_____

_____

_____

_____

_____

_____

_____

_____

_____

_____

_____

_____

_____

_____

_____

_____

_____

Chapter Three

𝒜 𝒟ᴏɢ's 𝐋ɪғᴇ

"Life is something that happens
when you can't get to sleep."
—Fran Lebowitz

Some days WOOFers ought to hit themselves over the head. We're so busy with everything and everybody else, we ignore the Alpha Dog...us.

To Read or Not To Read

Va-*roooooooom*...

My summer read hits the patio. Lemonade shoots up my nose. *Who's the Neanderthal with the leaf blower?* From my *lounge* chair, I glare at Mr. Perfect Home Turf. Death rays, however, can't penetrate his grass-covered goggles.

Clank! Crash!

Now what?

Spinning the other direction, I catch Mr. Manic Mechanic lobbing a bent hubcap into a metal trashcan which tips over and clatters down the driveway and out into the street causing a passing car to swerve (gasp), barely missing the trashcan *and* Mr. Perfect Home Turf's prize rosebush.

Grrrr... Stop already!

Yard work. Cleaning the garage. *What are ya'll thinking?*

Ah, now *she's* got the right idea—Sally, curled under the biggest shade tree on the block. The only energy she's expending is the occasional flick of her chocolate-colored tail to scatter flies off her back.

I mean, look at her. She's not crabby about all the crabgrass, guilt-ridden by a grocery list yellowing with age, or a planet suffering from its own form of hot flashes.

"What *a dog's life*, huh, Sal?"

WOOF!

"Well, hey, girl, what's the matter? Something wr..."

I'm slow, but now I get it. WOOF. *I'm a* WOOF*er, so I deserve to chill from time to time, too.*

"Sally, you're a *genius.*"

Making a mental note to save her the next hambone, I dust off my book and ease back into the chair.

A dog's life. Precisely...

d.d.dawg

WOOFers!

Let's keep our noses off the ground and check out the scenery ahead. We never know when we'll stumble upon a life-changing adventure.

Stepping Stones

Several years back, my husband and I, along with our adopted dog, Molly, vacationed in Maine at the summer home of long-time friends. The Northeast landscape was new to South Florida Molly, and she was captivated by the trees, the lake and the *unusual* scents.

Early the first morning, before I could snap Molly's leash, she took off running hell-bent after a fast-moving object; across the yard, and under the neighbor's shed. Two shrill barks and a yelp later, she crawled sheepishly from under the shed, her first odiferous encounter with a black and white striped "kitty cat," over...at least for her. For everyone else within 20 feet, the smell would linger on.

The cabin was on one of Maine's crystal clear lakes. Large rocks scattered outward from the shore, and, to Molly's aging eyes, must have appeared to extend to the edge of the earth. With the expertise of a mountain goat, she made her way from rock to rock, venturing ever farther, perhaps searching for the illusive loons that called early in the morning and just after sunset.

Molly had always investigated with her nose to the

ground, never seeming to care what lay ahead, only sensing the activity of the past. But, now, with eyes scanning the horizon and ears perked, she leaped from her comfort zone to explore the lake. *The heck with palm trees and white sand beaches, this is where my heart belongs.*

Being in her 50's (dog years) didn't stop Molly from embarking upon a new adventure.

And it won't stop me.

Milkbone

Charge!

Look what's in the mail—a Pet Rewards credit card application. Hmm, let me see...

Dear Molly,

Your pet is one of a kind...a loyal companion, funny performer, and trusted keeper of your closest secrets. So imagine being able to use your credit card to collect valuable "Reward" points! The more you charge, the more points you'll collect to buy toys, food, snacks and pet-care products for your faithful companion.

At the low, introductory rate of %#$@, you may charge up to three ka-zillion dollars and make your dear little Fluffy happy at the same time. Get the card that is as rewarding as your pet!

Interesting offer. But I can't apply even if I want to! It's made out to Molly...my dog!

And, I'm sure not putting a credit card in her paws. I can see it all now; piles of squeaky toys, gourmet dog food, climate-controlled doggie condo, her own cat to chase and torment.

Uh-uh. Not gonna happen. Sorry, Molly.

Milkbone

A True Friend Acts Like A Dog

A true friend is a WOOFer who will do anything she can to make you happy during your two-week visit with her. Even if it means getting on all fours and doing a pretty darn good impersonation (howls and all) of your beloved dog...simply because you miss him.

Milkbone

If reincarnation exists
I know that I have just one wish.
To come back as my pet
Would be good as it gets
'Cause I've made that dog's life total bliss!

Mad Dog

Are you leading a Dog's Life?
How so...

Women Only Over Fifty

Chapter Four

ARE WE BARKING UP THE WRONG TREE?

*"If I had to live my life again, I'd make the same mistakes,
only sooner."*
—Tallulah Bankhead

Part of the WOOFer daily creed is to keep a *paws*itive outlook when it comes to expanding waistlines, deepening wrinkles and muddled memories. But some days are just a little harder than others...

Maintaining PMA
*Paws*itive Meno*paws*al Attitude

 There they were on TV, three veterans of the Ladies' Professional Golf Association giving a public service announcement on the joys of meno*paws*. Now I was really getting sucked into PMA, *Positive Menopawsal Attitude,* until one of the ladies announced that going through meno*paws* doesn't mean your life is over. We could still have *more than one-third of our lives left.* Hmpft. Being a cup-half-empty gal, my immediate reaction was, "Good grief. My life is two-thirds *over.*"

 Responding to my frustration that I couldn't lose weight, my young, trim gynecologist asked, "How much weight do you think you need to lose?"

"At least 10 pounds."

"Well, then," she barked, "*lose 10 pounds.*"

🐾 Proud of recent efforts to watch my weight, I felt compelled to share my strategy with my husband. "I'm not sure if you've noticed," I beamed over dinner one night, "but I'm trying to cut down on calories by only filling one plate instead of having side dishes for vegetables and salad."

"I noticed," he remarked, "and must say, I have a lot of admiration for you."

A smug, satisfied smile crossed my face... until he added, "You must be closing in on the *Guinness Book of World Records* for the largest dinner plate."

🐾 With each advancing year, I'm realizing that if I want to "run with the big dogs," I can't just nap under the porch. As my metabolism slows, *Positive Menopawsal Attitude* isn't enough. In order to stay young, I just gotta keep those paws in motion!

So...I got one of those new-fangled walking machines a year ago Christmas and I'm getting plenty of exercise...dusting it.

🐾 I think I'm losing my identity. I began noticing it

after an experience with my basset hound. Everyone knew and loved Wilbur with his soulful eyes and lumbering gait, but few neighbors knew my name, or cared, other than I was the person at the end of his leash.

One morning an important package was due to arrive, but I had to get Wilbur to a vet appointment. I loaded all 70 pounds of him into the car and headed down the street, only to see the express mail truck parked a few doors away. Rolling to a stop, I called to the driver, identifying myself and asking if he had something for me.

"Yes, I do," he said, cautiously walking my direction. "But I can only deliver to an address...Oh, hi, *Wilbur!*"

Delivery complete.

🐾 A friend suffers from migraines. Many times they're brought on by squinting into the sun or by a bright, flashing light. (She spent the disco era in a dark, quiet room.) Just her luck when she passes to that *great reward*, the command to "Walk toward the light" will bring on another migraine.

🐾 WOOFers know when to let "sleeping dogs lie." Although not the preferred method of communication, a white lie is necessary in the case of certain questions:

✓ Have I gained weight?
✓ Are these scales ten pounds heavy?

✓ Does this plaid skirt I bought on sale and can't return make my butt look big?

✓ What do you think of my new *cranberry* hair color?

✓ Have I really changed *that* much since we met? (There is *no* right answer to this question.)

🐾 Who hasn't stressed over those yearly mammograms. Don't know about you, but I just love standing tippy-toes while leaning at a 90-degree angle as some perky-chested technician smashes *my* breasts into a couple of Sunday morning pancakes.

Milkbone

Petting furry animals has been proven to lower blood pressure, resulting in less stress and more contentment.

Covers

On
Off
On
Off
Turn
Toss
Turn
Toss
Eyes
Open
Close
Open
Stare. Stare. Stare.

Thoughts curnin' 'round
Like a tilt-a-whirl.
Oh, the restless night
Of a meno*paws*al girl.

All this lack of sleep,
Makes me such a bitch.
Dark circles 'round my eyes
Make me look just like a witch!

I'd hide out if I could
Tucked in my bed all day,

Beneath a spread, a quilt,
Or a downy-filled duvet.

But once this "change" subsides
I'll be back to being me—
The sweet and loving gal
That I always used to be.

Oh, you say those days are gone?
"Hot" has a whole new spin?
I really need some sleep, but...
Here the covers go again!

On
      Off
On
        Off …

d.d.dawg

WOOFers Present When Flashing

They're a Godsend, those bright orange signs along construction zones: *Workers Present When Flashing.* I'd hate to miss even *one* handsome, buffed worker "flashing"—muscles chiseled like Adonis, sweat collecting on his back....

No, wait. I mean, as a responsible driver, I value knowing when a fully-clothed, hardworking construction guy's on the job, so I don't hit on ...uh, I mean, *hit* him.

Oh, the accidents and ill-fated encounters avoided thanks to those signs. Maybe there's something to be learned when it comes to run-ins with WOOFers. Case in point.

My husband awoke one night to find me throwing off the bedcovers. "Are you flashing?"

"Flashing?" I barked. "You think I'm *flashing* you?"

"Uh, no, dear...I mean are you *hot* flashing?"

Whatever. It's gonna happen. Without fair warning, people *will* unwittingly cross into the danger zone of meno*pawsal* WOOFers. Therefore, at the time of doctor's confirmation, WOOFers must be issued T-shirts printed with the following:

d.d.dawg

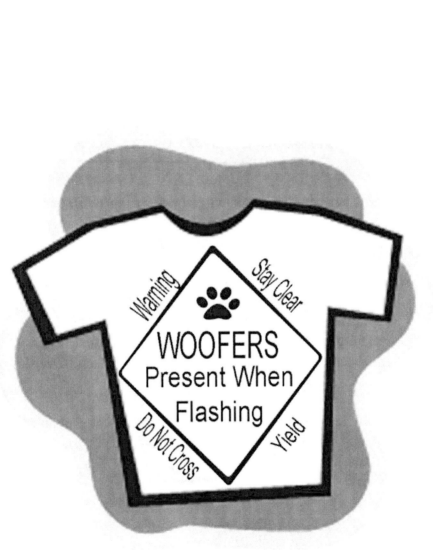

Sometimes It's Hard To Be a Woman

Those immortal words of Tammy Wynette are even more meaningful after you hit the big 5-0.

Let's start with the day you get the news you're officially in meno*paws*. In my case, the doctor called to inform me that my hormones were "totally whacked out." *Whacked out*? Now where did we learn this medical term?

Okay, I'll deal with it. Then he recited all the other joys of meno*paws*—mood swings; memory something, oh, loss; weight gain; loss of muscle tone; the risk of osteoporosis and heart disease; diminished sex drive, etc. etc. Deep breath. *I'm a strong woman. I can handle it.*

Then sleep deprivation kicks in. It's 3 am—my mind's racing, my body's collapsing, my husband's snoring sounds like a freight train roaring past my head, and I begin to doubt my reason for living.

But about the time I'm at my wits end with this meno*paw*sal thing, I hear good news on my favorite morning show. "*…as they age, women lose fat on the balls of their feet.*"

Ah, ha! Proof that in at least one respect I'm as good as I used to be. In fact—I'm better. We're *all* better. We're *losing fat.*

Doggone, we're still good! Let's scoff at those thickening waists and fuzzy memories. We'll let our feet do the talking. As we age, we *lose fat. (Okay, okay, so it's just on the balls of our feet...)*

Mad Dog

Mad Dog

My gyno told me, "You better bone up.
You've hit meno*paws* *a*nd WOOFers ain't pups.

"Eat rabbit food. Drink non-fat milkshakes.
Walk till you drop And try to lose weight."

I snarled at the doctor, baring my teeth,
Till my bladder barked, g*et rid of this tea.*

I ran down the hall to the Ladies Room sign.
But two women yapped, "Back of the line."

I flagged down a nurse. "I'm gonna blow!"
But she thought I meant my water just broke.

Then one lady gasped, "How could *we* know?
She's not *that* big and she is kind of old."

Diuretically doomed, I tried to speak.
But each time I did, a nurse said, "Just breathe…"

Finally my doctor was called to the room.
He said, "What the heck's the matter with you?"

I pulled at his tie and said, "Read my lips.
I need a bed pan and not these stirrups!"

The doctor ran out. He yelled, "She's insane!"
That's when the men in white coats walked in.

I begged, "If I promise to eat right and jog,
Will you stop thinking that I'm a *mad dog*?"

They canceled Code Blue, so my bladder and me
Dashed to the toilet—there was no T P.
d.d.dawg

I can still feel my fire light
Each evening around midnight.
It's only because
I'm in meno*paws*
Hot flashes now make me ignite!

Mad Dog

Ever feel like you're barking up the wrong tree? Come on, let us have it!

Chapter Five

The Wonderful World of WOOF Theme Park

"Girls just like to have fun."
—Cyndi Lauper

When it comes right down to it, WOOFers are puppies at heart...Sooo, why not create our very own amusement park?

Hair-Raising Roller Coaster—Do you have problem hair? Is it limp and lifeless? Ride our hair-raising roller coaster and get instantaneous body. You'll step back onto terra firma with a head of hair that would make Marge Simpson proud.

Hot-Flash Ferris Wheel—If hot flashes have you sweating like a stroll in the Sahara, take a seat on our specially designed Ferris wheel. With every 360-degree turn, you'll get drenched with our standard-issue fire hose. We guarantee to drop your body temperature 10 degrees or your money back.

Meno*paws* Merry-Go-Round—Does meno*paws* have you running around in circles? Is your life filled with too many ups and downs? Then it's time for a spin on our meno*paws* merry-go-round. You'll get so dizzy and disoriented, when the ride's over, you'll feel perfectly normal.

Far-From-Reality Fun House—*Woof* down those hot dogs and that cotton candy. Devour those funnel cakes and ice cream bars without fear of middle-age spread. You'll be able to stand, with confidence, in front of our fun house mirrors. They're specially cut to take off 30 pounds. (Get there early…It fills up fast.)

Monster Mood Swings — Is your disposition changing faster than women's shoe styles? Check out our fabulous new giant swings. For 15 equilibrium-deprived minutes, you'll swing back and forth...back and forth...*back and forth,* until the only "mood" you'll be in is queasy.

Bozo Bumper Cars—Get rid of suppressed anger in our bumper cars. We'll arrange, in strategic positions, life-size cutouts of your former hairdresser, your idiot boss, your exes or perhaps that snobby clerk at the *Foo-Foo Boutique* who turned her back when you walked in wearing your favorite sweat suit. Bump those bozos 'til all your hidden hostilities are a thing of the past.

Chocolate Choo-Choo—If you've walked more than a few feet, you're probably tired. Climb aboard our chocolate choo-choo train. As you take in the sights and sounds of WOOF Park, you will delight in biting pieces of *real chocolate* off the train. Don't get carried away, though. Leave enough train to make it back to the station. (Warning: Seats melt during hot flashes.)

Milkbone

I wish meno*paws* could be like
A theme park with lots of wild rides.
I'd just have to pay
For one crazy day
Then go back to my nice normal life!

Mad Dog

Holler Coaster

Amusement rides scare the pants off me. But there's this one...About as close to a roller coaster as I ever get. So I climb aboard, knees shaky, palms sweaty, and place a death grip on the safety bar in the back "car." In front of me sits a child I suspect stood on tiptoes to measure "tall enough."

Slowly the ride kicks into motion, and I shriek at the top of my lungs! My *vocals* heighten with every ascent and downward swoop, and shrill sharply around each s-curve.

Back, safe and "sound," and proud as punch, I wobble down the exit ramp behind the little girl.

"So, sweetheart," her mother asks, "how did you like the ride?"

"Well, *it* was great," the munchkin says, "but the woman behind me screamed in my ears the whole time!"

d.d.dawg

*What's the most fun thing you do,
and when did you last do it?*

_____

_____
_____
_____
_____
_____
_____
_____
_____
_____
_____
_____
_____
_____
_____
_____
_____
_____
_____

_____
_____
_____
_____
_____
_____
_____
_____
_____
_____
_____
_____
_____
_____
_____
_____
_____
_____
_____
_____
_____
_____
_____
_____
_____
_____
_____
_____

Chapter Six

ᵽᵾᵽᵽᵞ Cᕼᕼᕼᕼ

PUPPY CHOW

"I don't even butter my bread. I consider that cooking."
—Katherine Cebrian

WOOFers Restaurant

After a frolic-filled day at WOOF Theme Park, who wants to cook? Chow down at **WOOFers**.

WOOFers

♦ Open to women only over 50 (and cute male escorts in tight jeans).

♦ Casual dining…over-sized shirts, comfortable shoes and elastic waistbands required.

♦ Tables include electric fans and extra ice water for those hot flash emergencies.

♦ Equipped with extra potties. No need to wait in line when the bladder says, "Now!" And positively *no mirrors*.

♦ Where dessert is mandatory, and you'll never find the words, diet, low-fat, or calorie-counter. Doggie Bags supplied at no extra charge.

Senior Maintenance Menu

Woof It Down
Main Dishes

Howlin' Ham—*ham with extra spicy sauce*
Mutt Loaf—*just like Mom used to make*
Shepherd's Pie—*enough for the whole litter*
Tail Between the Legs—*T-bone steak & fried chicken*

Three Dogs, a Cow, a Pig, and a Turkey
Deluxe or Bite-size

Mutt Dog—*hot dog loaded with everything*
Top Dog—*hot dog loaded with everything plus chili*
Bowser Burger—*so loaded it'll keep your tummy barking*
One Leg Up—*open faced ham or turkey sandwich*
That Dog Won't Hunt—*hot dog with mustard only*

Pick Of the Litter
Bread, Salads and Side Items

Pure Bred—*real homemade bread*
Puppy Potatoes—*new potatoes smothered in real butter*
French Poodle Fries—*fried with the skins on*
Roll-Over Onion Rings—*our chef cries real tears*
Dog House Dills—*huge crunchy old-fashioned dills*
X-tra Crunchy Dog House Dills—*fried dill pickles that'll make you sit up and bark*
Maxaroni & Cheese—*an old favorite with tons of real cheddar*

Growlin' Greens—*a salad so loaded with bad stuff that it actually tastes good*
Furry Fruit Plate—*fresh fruit topped with coconut*
Mad Dog Fruit Plate—*fresh fruit with real whipped cream*

Lap 'Em Up, Lassies
Beverages

Walkin' the Dog—*beverage of your choice (so big you'll visit the 'Lassie Room' often)*
Sassie Lassie—*Bloody Mary with a dash of Tabasco*
Canine Cadillac—*sinfully good crème de menthe over crushed ice*
See Spot Run—*a drink to remind you why you cut back*
Tail Chaser—*a drink to remind you why you quit*

Drooling Desserts
No further explanation needed

Pedigree Pies—*blue ribbon pies loaded with fruit and sugar*
Bone Appe´tit—*homemade vanilla ice cream*
Speckled Pups—*bite-size chocolate chip cookies*
Drooling Dreamsicles—*melt all the way down your collar*
Bowser Brigade—*three desserts (your choice) on one plate*
Paws 'n Claws—*coffee and warm sweet rolls*
WOOFer's Best Friend—*anything chocolate*

*Proprietors: d.d dawg, MadDog, & Milkbone
(Not responsible for weight gain.)*

Spice of Life

There comes a point in every over-fifty woman's life when there's no denying she's a WOOFer. I should have suspected my time would involve food.

The cafe's soup de jour was to die for. On and on I raved about the flavor.

"Could the spicy seasoning be," I wondered aloud, "canine pepper?"

It wasn't so much that I mistakenly said "canine" instead of cayenne, but that until my husband laughed, I hadn't even noticed.

d.d. dawg

A Bone to Pick!

Being asked if you qualify for the senior citizen discount. **Not** being asked if you qualify for the senior citizen discount.

Remembering Rhubarb Pie

My grandmother taught me how to bake pie, and so much more…

My grandmother lived "down by the creek" in our small home town, and tended an award-winning garden. Each year she'd grow corn, green beans, tomatoes, cucumbers, green peppers, cabbage, fresh mint and much, much more. Most of which appeared daily on her kitchen table.

But, best of all…she grew rhubarb. May Rainbolt was the finest rhubarb pie baker in the county, which was proven by the stash of county fair blue ribbons she kept "inconspicuously" in an old Ball canning jar on the windowsill. "Oh, pshaw." She'd blush. "Those old things? I'm just saving them for quilt scraps."

When she wasn't gathering blue ribbons at the Harrison County Fair, we'd spend hours together playing bingo under a dusty tent on the Midway, competing for "valuable" prizes. My biggest thrill was winning a rainbow-striped pitcher and matching iced-tea glasses. I'm not sure whether the tears in my grandmother's eyes were from joy at the sight of my gift, or from wondering where in the world she was going to store another set of worthless glassware.

She lived well into her 70's, but in my family, that's like being struck down in the prime of life. Still, she taught me a lesson—one I value to this day. The best piecrust* is made with vinegar. Yes...*vinegar*.

But the most important thing I learned from my grandmother is that sometimes, especially on a steamy, Southern Indiana afternoon, nothing beats sitting on the front porch, rocking gently back and forth in the swing.

Add a slice of warm, rhubarb pie...and it's perfect.

*Vinegar Pie Crust

1/3 cup cold water
2 T vinegar
1 egg
1 tsp. salt
1 cup & 3 T shortening
3 cups flour

Cream first 5 ingredients
Add flour and mix until moistened
(Double crust pie)

Milkbone

I used to eat everything in sight
And my clothes never fit too tight.
Now I can gain weight
Just glancing at cake
Without savoring one tasty bite!

Mad Dog

What's your favorite food, and how does it make you feel when you eat it?

_____
_____
_____
_____
_____
_____
_____
_____
_____
_____
_____
_____
_____
_____
_____
_____
_____
_____
_____
_____
_____
_____
_____
_____
_____
_____

Chapter Seven

OLD DOG/NEW TRICKS

"I was going to have plastic surgery until I noticed the doctor's office was full of portraits by Picasso."
—Rita Rudner

Comes as no surprise to the over-50 woman that reinventing the wheel is a waste of time and energy. One must instead, ever so carefully, re*align* it. A skill WOOFers practically invented!

Dog Ma

Just when you think you know someone, they throw you a curve.

She didn't drink, swear or gamble.

She didn't gossip or speak ill of anyone.

She went to church regularly, volunteered and helped the needy.

She raised eight children to become responsible adults.

How was I to know? I mean, when we walked into the grocery, I was as certain of my 70-year-old mother-in-law's reactions in *any* circumstance as I was that the sun would set that evening…and that it would be in the west.

Even when her neighbor cornered us on the dairy aisle, I suspected nothing. Mom managed a cordial conversation while the woman whined about high milk prices and late mail delivery.

Respectfully squeezing in a word, Mom introduced me to the woman, and it hit me. She was the one who'd nearly had a coronary earlier in the week, complaining that my toy poodle had trespassed her "prized" yard and left more than dog tracks.

Mom, with her usual poise and grace, called the woman's attention to another neighbor eyeing the cottage cheese specials, and quietly steered me toward checkout. The grocery doors barely closed behind us when she tugged my elbow. "Hurry. Before she gets home. We've got to get back and let Pompy out so he can sh** all over her yard!"

d.d.dawg

Ode To The Cell Phone

I used to think cell phones were so dumb.
Who needs to talk while on the run?
In a checkout line I'd steam and stew.
How could that person be so rude?
I was tempted to say, "Please just shut up.
I don't need to hear all your personal stuff!"
Behind some fool who couldn't steer,
I'd shout, "Get that thing off your ear!"
But I have to admit, with a sheepish grin,
I, too, am guilty now and then.
I've learned how to put my Blue Tooth on.
And my ring is a favorite downloaded song.
I text the grandkids, though I'm really slow,
And return my calls while on the go.
But I try not to be the one who's cursed
Because I have a ringing purse.
You're never too old for technology.
Just use some doggone courtesy!

Mad Dog

When I was young in the 60s
I wanted to be a real hippie.
The closest I came
was growing my mane,
Saying "far-out" and acting real dippy!

Mad Dog

An Oxy-moron

It's said time races for those of us over 50 because we're on the "downhill" run.

Based on that "coastal" theory, one might ask: Why, then, do we drive slower than we did in our younger days? Shouldn't the momentum increase our speed?

Alas, a contradiction.

Which brings me to a greeting I received the other day from a young motorist hugging my tailpipe. "Moron!!!" he screamed as he whipped around me, punctuating his remark with a honk of his horn.

Young man! I knowingly smiled and waved. *I'm not just* any *moron!*

Time flies. I creep. That qualifies me as an OXY-moron.

Kids. What they don't know.

d.d.dawg

Why They Call It a Cursor

Like many women over 50, I'm "technologically challenged." I've come a long way for someone born before her parents got their first TV, but still get frustrated when modern technology goes haywire. And when it gets personal, it means war.

Take my computer (please). I cheerfully log on one morning and then zap! A threatening tone and a big red X appears on the monitor. The words, "What is this?" are plastered across my kittens-at-play screen saver. What do you mean "What is this?" How the heck do I know? All I did was turn you on, you idiot computer. Don't tell me you won't work. You worked fine yesterday. So what's your problem this morning?

No answer, hmmm? So, I start over or—reboot—as they say in computer lingo. Reboot? What if I reboot you out the door? But I resist that temptation for the moment. My computer restarts and is magically back on track despite the fact that I did nothing different this time. Go figure.

Next I encounter a roadblock creating an outline. You know—the ones we did in school with Roman numerals. I try to add a capital "A" under Roman numeral "I," and Word fights me by adding the "II." Hey—I know when I want to add the "II" and it ain't now. Talk about who is really stupid. Or is that *whom?*

I give up on the outline and decide to answer a few e-mails entering the password I've had for 10 years. "Password incorrect. Have your forgotten your password?" I don't think so! I type the exact same word again and you guessed it. It works. Take that, computer.

The anti-virus program, designed to prevent my computer from getting "sick," flares up with a warning that a Trojan horse, aka "really sneaky virus" has been detected. Ok—at least you found it, but if you're so brilliant, why do you let these viruses in at all? Oh, I get it; the 14-year-old virus-creating-geek, who rarely leaves his basement bedroom and his precious laptop, is more intelligent than any computer or program.

I'm exhausted from the morning's technology challenges. This Windows operating system designed to make my computer more "user friendly," has me thinking unfriendly thoughts. *How about I just toss you out the window?* I'm spewing a string of #*%$ words ...which explains why the little arrow on my computer screen is called a *cursor!*

Mad Dog

Two Tuesdays

If I could have two Tuesdays,
I'd really get things done.
I'd work my fingers to the bone
Then, next day, have some fun.

If I could have two Tuesdays,
I wouldn't have to say,
"How can it be twelve o'clock?
I've lost another day!"

If I could have two Tuesdays,
I'd write and write and write.
And, then on *Tuesday,* I'd be free
To watch TV all night.

If I could have two Tuesdays,
How happy I would be.
I'd clean the house on Tuesday,
And, then have my Tuesday free.

If I could have two Tuesdays,
I'd finally clear my desk
of all those yellow sticky notes.
They create such a mess!

If I could have two Tuesdays,
I wouldn't have to wait,
To sit outside, or take a walk,
Or simply meditate.

Now… it's my *second* Tuesday.
But, I've had so much to do,
How did it get to be so late?
I never will get through!

If I could have two *Wednesdays*…

Milkbone

Big Macs, Jack Daniels, and Rock 'n Roll.
On some of us they've taken their toll.
But those who've survived
Are living their lives
With veggies, green tea and Dr. Scholl's.

Mad Dog

"Readers" Beware

Oh, what a bea-U-tiful morning! Sun's streaming through the bathroom skylight, shower spray's relaxing my shoulders, and I've got a yummy new hair product to tr...*ACK!* Do I leave it on 5 minutes or...an hour? *Where are my glasses? What am I gonna do? What am I gonna do?*

I hold the bottle up to my nose, at the end of my arms, over my right shoulder, under my left knee... "I give up." Slumped against the wet tiles, I'm sinking... sinking... sinking... But what's this? These water droplets collecting on my eyelashes? They're ... they're refracting the light in the most peculiar way. *So* peculiar, the fine print's coming into focus.

A lifesaver. And *now* I know what to do when I'm dining out and my "readers" are in my other purse. Request a large pitcher of water, and, while perusing the menu, pour it over my head.

d.d.dawg

Experts say that having quality sex on a regular basis will take nine years off your biological age...no matter what position you use!

List a few new tricks you could teach some old dogs you know.

_____
_____
_____
_____
_____
_____
_____
_____
_____
_____
_____
_____
_____
_____
_____
_____
_____
_____
_____
_____
_____
_____
_____
_____
_____
_____

Chapter Eight

Putting On The Dog

"I base my fashion taste on what doesn't itch."
—Gilda Radner

As the female population ages, magazines feature more and more fetching fashions for the 50+ woman. While recognizing their efforts, we dug up some helpful hints of our own.

How to Dress the Mature Mutt

 Wear bright colors, especially from the waist up. They light up the face and help WOOFers avoid that dog-tired look.

 Boots for fall and winter help hide unsightly varicose veins. They look great on the old paws, too. But, a warning: Be sure they're roomy enough for those bunions.

 Spandex undergarments help pull in unwanted bulges and hide extra pounds.

If your "Sharpei neck" is a problem, wear that good ol' standby, a *turtleneck*. Or, a nice silver or turquoise choker is always an option.

 Avoid sleeveless dresses and tops if your upper arms wave goodbye after you do.

 Low-heeled shoes and sandals are not only flattering, they can keep a WOOFer's *dogs* from barking after a long day.

 A push up bra can do wonders for the over-50 upper body. And a little cleavage will make those old hounds pant.

 Color-coordinated headscarves are a good idea for those car rides when you have the uncontrollable urge to hang your head out the window.

 In the winter months, it's a good idea to periodically wear snug-fitting jeans to force you to confront your weight. Those stretchy denim leggings and sweatshirts have a tendency to get a *little* too comfortable.

 Although jewelry dresses up most any outfit, the WOOFer must be careful when wearing dangling earrings or necklaces. It can be most embarrassing when you drag them in your food dish.

Capris are considered a no-no for the mature mutt, but we find them to be most comfy. Especially since they cover up that droopy knee fat. Besides, if they were good enough for Laura Petrie, they're good enough for us.

Mad Dog & Milkbone

Mirror

Mirror, mirror, in my vanity drawer,
Dare I gaze at you anymore?
Or shall I leave you right where you are
In a place easy to ignore.

Lately when I look at you,
I swear, I swear I don't know who
Is looking back,
Who's looking back at who!

Sometimes Mother, like a Cheshire cat,
Slowly disappearing, smiling back.
But then some days I catch a glimpse
Of this one ageless fact:

Mirror, mirror, I adore
Can't hold me captive anymore,
If I place my vanity
Beside it in the drawer.

d.d.dawg

The Saturn Diet

Enough already with "Men are from Mars. Women are from Venus!" Give me a break.

I wanna be from Saturn!

What? You haven't heard the latest?

Saturn is denser than Earth. Therefore, a 150-pound woman would only weigh 135! Whoo-hoo! Bring back my 1980s closet.

I dream of zipping up those size 8 Liz Claiborne jeans. Slipping on my L. L. Bean cargo shorts and tank top. Oh, and my two-piece bathing suit! How great would it be to *slowly* remove my beach robe and not have to sprint Olympic-style into the pool. Instead, I could proudly stroll, sit on the edge, and gracefully slink into the water without fear of being mistaken for a beached whale.

Okay...where do you buy tickets for the space shuttle?

Milkbone

Now that I'm in middle age
I must say I've noticed some change.
My waist has expanded.
My eyebrows disbanded.
And I have a much lower "backstage."

Mad Dog

WOOF

A Sign of the Times

We've roamed this earthly plane
For over 50 years.
To celebrate, let's all tattoo
Our southern hemispheres.

A simple WOOFer emblem:
Paws on our derrieres,
Might be a nice indulgence, "butt"
Just who will see it there?

Still, maybe doggie bones
So proudly we'll display,
Reminding us we need to take
Our calcium each day.

But, what happens to tattoos
As skin begins to age?
Symbols look distorted stamped
Upon a wrinkled page.

Ah, best to leave tattoos for
The young "graffiti" set.
So there won't be a reason that
We'll look "back" with regret!

d.d.dawg

Oh, thanks, I think...

On a recent trip, I indulged in the hotel breakfast bar. I walked into the room and immediately noticed a pair of eyes checking me out. Figuring it was some random act of curiosity, I poured a cup of coffee, added condiments and worked my way to an empty table.

The eyes were still on me! Accompanied by a smile! And this was no *geezer*, mind you. Glancing over a *USA Today* was a 30-something, handsome hunk.

Well, this 50-something "girl" was feeling a little flirty, so I smiled back, resisting the urge to bat my eyelashes as well. (Didn't want him choking on his bagel.)

After breakfast I decided to get coffee for the road. As luck would have it, my young "friend" had the same idea and walked up behind me. As I filled my cup, I tried to think of something witty to say, but he spoke first.

"I just wanted you to know how much I admire senior citizens who aren't afraid to dress stylishly. Have a nice day!" He smiled, filled a travel mug, and walked out of the lounge, leaving me with *figurative* egg on my face.

Milkbone

98

If you could wear anything you wanted, what would it be, and have you ever worn it?

_____

_____

_____

_____

_____

_____

_____

_____

_____

_____

_____

_____

_____

_____

_____

_____

_____

_____

_____

Chapter Nine

Every Dog Has Her Day

"There are worse things than looking stupid.
Sleeping through life is one of them."
—Laura Preble

We've tallied the number of days it takes to become an official WOOFer—18,250 (not counting leap years). Whew! Anyway, each and every one was significant in its own way. And, some days were special because they were shared with special people.

My Grandmother's Hands

I glance at the computer keyboard and recoil in horror. My grandmother's hands are resting there! Attached to *my* wrists! Yep, it's them alright—wrinkled with age spots and the same osteoarthritis-gnarled knuckles that to me, as a child, had looked so fascinating. Well, they don't look so darn fascinating *now*!

How did this happen? I went to bed with the silky smooth hands of a *young* fifty-*ish* year-old, and woke up with purple, pitted prune hands and knobby fingers!

I grab the *industrial strength, advanced healing, super-hydrating* hand cream and nearly exhaust the contents of a

10-ounce bottle. There. That should do it. Feeling the lotion soaking into my bone-dry skin and swollen knuckles, I reflect on the idea of bringing back my grandmother's white gloves...*vogue* in the 40s and 50s.

Realizing this is probably not an option, my mind shifts from vanity to thoughts of my grandmother and the many delightful summers spent at her house. I picture...

Her hands plucking the delicate blooms off the petunias, and showing me how to pick them off without damaging the rest of the plant.

Her hands dishing out homemade ice cream and giant-size servings of her delicious white cake topped with buttery caramel icing.

Her hands dealing a deck of cards and patiently teaching me how to play canasta.

Her hands holding a fluffy, warm towel as she greeted a shivering five-year-old wading out of the shallow creek that ran behind her house.

Maybe I'm over-reacting. After all, the love in my grandmother's hands is a far more cherished and lasting memory than their superficial appearance.

Looking again at the keyboard, I flex my fingers—warmth spreading through each one, holding the precious memory of my grandmother's hands.

Milkbone

Getting old will be such a drag
If I turn into an old hag.
So, a smile I'll project
To say that, by heck,
I'm gonna be one happy old bag!

Mad Dog

My Turn

To think I yelp about my life, how at this age I deserve to be thrown a few more bones...

Nestled between sweet-smelling sheets, I'd spy her reaching for a frayed copy of *Heidi* or *The Bobbsey Twins*. "One of your *picture* stories, okay?" My gaze settled just above her head. There, amid old flowery wallpaper, dangled my favorite picture—the faded likeness of an old English farmhouse.

With a twinkle in her blue eyes, she'd sit on the edge of the lumpy mattress and transport herself—and a little girl with big expectations—into a magical world of make-believe.

I hung on my grandmother's every word. Why that straw-laden cart stood abandoned among the chickens. What the family laughed about over dinner, there behind the ivy-framed door. What games the children played beneath the thatched roof.

Little did I know what a struggle real life was for Grandmother.

She washed other people's dirty clothes. Her 50-plus-year-old body wrestled a wringer washer and lugged baskets of wet laundry outdoors to dry. Or, during inclement weather, draped them on a wooden "dryer" propped around a pot-belly stove (one that warmed her meals and had a ravenous appetite for chopped wood). She ironed—to perfection—everything from socks to heavily-starched white shirts, even on days when the thermometer neared 100 degrees, the only relief a fan that circulated hot air.

She scraped dirty food trays and operated a steamy dishwasher in the school cafeteria. She changed hundreds of dirty diapers, babysitting so late that her white hair often didn't hit the pillow until after midnight. And she boarded a grimy bus to move north when her son's wife died. She knew firsthand the challenges of being a single parent—her husband having been murdered in cold blood when she was in her 20's leaving her with two small children.

That dime-store picture worthy of a thousand of my grandmother's words vanished years ago. I now treasure a black-and-white snapshot of her standing in front of the dilapidated sheds on our property, smiling beside her prized flowerbed.

Never one to say much about her own life, it's my turn:

In a small, historic town in Southern Indiana, on the

banks of Big Indian Creek, lived a quietly courageous woman, Lulu Pearl Quebbeman Lord...

d.d.dawg

My age and my weight are not little
But I like this life in the middle.
No pregnancy scares
Or teenage nightmares
And finally I have time to piddle.

Mad Dog

In Continent

Woofers sometimes find the most frequent trips they make are to the bathroom, still we can venture to far corners of the earth... and have experiences they don't put in the travel brochures.

South Africa is a country of 11 official languages. I have trouble enough with American dialects, let alone English generously peppered with Zulu or Xhosa. So most of my two-week sojourn was spent listening carefully to what was said and repeating myself often.

But on my final day there, checking out at a guesthouse, I discovered some conversations need little translation. Call them Universal, if you will.

"Give me your phone number."

I looked over my shoulder to see the young man who served us a perfect breakfast each morning, in spite of the slight language barrier.

"My phone number? I live in the States."

"Give me your phone number." He smiled big. "I will call

you."

So I did. Quickly. "770-....." He bowed and went about his duties. Don't know if he just wanted the satisfaction of having a foreigner's number, or he was delivering a pickup line because he thought I was hot.

Yeah, that has to be it. He thought I was hot. A hot *dog.*

d.d.dawg

Just a Smile Away

Some of us face our greatest challenges in our 50's.
For me it was the sudden loss of my husband.

I knew that my husband, Sid, would probably die first, but I thought we'd be in our 80's. I was devastated when he died from a sudden heart attack just before his 57th birthday. We'd been married for almost 38 years and were best friends as well as soul mates.

For a long time after Sid's death, I merely existed—just going through the motions of everyday living.

The road to healing and recovery was painfully slow and often included taking three steps back for each two steps I managed to inch forward. But along the way I had so much love and support to keep me going. I also explored new interests, joined a grief group and developed new "common ground" friendships with other widows.

As strange as it sounds, Sid also kept me going. I often felt his warm presence encouraging me to move forward and find a new life. My grief counselor described it as the "new normal." It wasn't what you planned or wanted, but it was what you had. And part of the healing process included finding a way to accept the fact that my old life was gone—although not forgotten.

That brought up a whole new set of problems. How do you deal with the balance between treasuring those wonderful memories while making new ones? There were so many challenges that I never even considered, like "happiness guilt" and the difficult transition from being a married woman to a single one.

I was anxious to find something good about Sid's death. And I did. I grew as a person and conquered some of my fears like handling financial issues and being alone.

Two years have gone by since I experienced the worst day of my life. I look back and see that I've made progress and worked hard to make a new life. I know in my heart that he would be proud of me. Sometimes I still ask myself, "How am I supposed to live without you?" And Sid answers by telling me that he will always be in my heart—just a smile away.

Mad Dog

When the Last One Leaves the Litter

I can do my nails.
I have time for my
spouse,
In my empty nest,
This quiet house.

The dishes are done.
The house is clean.
I even fixed
The washing machine.

Now we can make love
Without any fear
The kids will wake up
And they will hear.

There once was a time,
With a kid on each leg,
I could mop the floor
While frying an egg.

Now the children are
gone.
They're all on their own.
We no longer have
A child proof home.

No PTA,
Drawings on the fridge.
No one to scream,
"But he did it!"

Yet I still wake,
On the darkest nights,
I swear that I hear
A small child cry.

There's no one to
comfort.
I go back to sleep.
I used to wish for
This kind of peace.

There's so much to like
About this time.
Now I can enjoy
My very own life.

Yet there are those
moments
I can't ignore
When I miss little things
That I had before.

Mad Dog

Every WOOFer's been changed by a person or event. What has altered your life?

Women Only Over Fifty

Chapter Ten

ꝑꝉꝶꝉꝕꝞꝭꝒ ꝑꝹꝉꝒꝹꝸꝞꝶꝋ

*"I want all my senses engaged.
Let me absorb the world's variety and uniqueness."*
—Maya Angelou

A *litter* bit of this and a *litter* bit of that.

Let Sleeping Dogs Lie

*I found out that old habits die hard
when you can't let sleeping dogs (or dog hair) lie.*

8:00 am: It's my 56th birthday. It's Thursday. As long as I can remember, Thursday is cleaning day. *Grrrrr.* Here's a wild and crazy idea...I'll go on strike. Not gonna cook. Not gonna clean, or do laundry. I'm not even gonna make the bed. One special Thursday just for me.

9:00 am: First thing on my agenda: Fix a cup of tea and relax. Whoa! Better clean the counter top before I contaminate the tea bag. Might as well do the sink and the stovetop while I have the anti-bacterial cleaner out. Now where is my favorite teacup? Oh, yeah. I ran the dishwasher last night. Here it is! Sparkling clean. Maybe I'll just put the rest of the dishes away.

10:30 am: Ah, nothing beats watching an old movie classic and relaxing on the sofa with a nice cup of *Earl Grey*. Whoa! Look at the dog hair! Better brush it off before I sit down. Hmmm… Guess it would be easier to get out the vacuum. Might as well quickly sweep the rug and the stairway while I'm at it. Maybe I'll take the vacuum upstairs and…

1:00 pm: Brilliant idea! I'll crawl back in bed and try to finish that book I started six months ago. Maybe I should go ahead and make the bed. Nope! Not gonna do it. I'll just arrange the pillows a little and smooth out the spread…

1:30 pm: Finally I can rest, read, or stare out at the beautiful blooms on the tulip tree. Man! That window is disgusting! Now, where did I put the Windex? Oh, good grief. Clean one window and the others look even worse! *Aaack!* I'll wash them all, and then take it easy for the rest of the day. Yep! That's the plan!

3:15 pm: That took a little longer than expected. Couldn't have clean windows and dirty screens. Must admit that although I used up a little excess energy, the payoff was worth it. Seeing the sun shining brightly through nice clean…Where did all this dust come from? *Sigh.* Where's the furniture polish?

6:30 pm: Oh, tummy's growling a little. Think I'll make a Caesar salad and add a few slices of that leftover chicken.

That's simple enough. *Ewww!* How long has this Romaine been in the crisper? Weeks, months, *years*? And I don't even want to know what's in those plastic containers! Off to the grocery.

8:00 pm: Calgon, take me away! A nice soothing soak is just the ticket...*if* I had remembered to clean the tub after giving the dog a bath...*Grrrrr*

Milkbone

Some days you're the dog.
Some days you're the hydrant.
Some days it's hard to know the difference.

d.d.dawg

A Bunch of Bones to Pick

The first car you ever owned now displays an *antique* license plate.

Those mood swings. One minute you're man's best friend—the next you want to sink your canines into his pants cuff.

Starving for weeks, eating nothing representing enjoyment or taste, you gain two pounds. Hubby loses three by waving a carrot stick under his nose.

Those boutique mirrors that make your size 12 body look like a size 8 until you get home and reality hits...in front of a *real* mirror.

Your new car costs twice as much as the first house you bought.

Gravity — your once fairly decent looking breasts are now closer to your hips than to your chin.

Unfortunately, those ridiculous health insurance premiums start to pay off.

Your kids call at 9:00 pm and ask, "Did I wake you?" And they did.

Faux Paws

***WOOFers** have discovered that as we age we often find ourselves in very awkward and socially unacceptable situations. We've gathered a few No-No's.*

A FAUX PAW is being invited out for a lovely afternoon on the 50-foot sailboat of your husband's boss, only to spend the next three hours *sick as a dog* barfing over the side!

A FAUX PAW is inviting your best friend and her husband to your house by saying, "We didn't want to do anything tonight. Wanna come over?"

A FAUX PAW is asking a guest at your son's wedding when her baby is due, only to hear her coldly reply that the baby is two months old.

A FAUX PAW is christening your friend's new *beige* sofa by spilling an entire glass of RED wine all over it.

A FAUX PAW is your husband referring to his *ex*-wife as his *other* wife.

A FAUX PAW is leaving a public ladies room with the paper seat protector stuck to your shoe.

A FAUX PAW is dancing the Twist at your granddaughter's 10th birthday party.

A FAUX PAW is dining out and sticking your finger in a stranger's bowl of soup to see if it tastes as good as it smells.

A FAUX PAW is mentioning an acquaintance's first name, how she *hates* it and is having it changed, to then remember the woman you're talking to has the *same* name.

A FAUX PAW is asking a friend who normally wears jeans and a sweatshirt, "Hey, what's with the dress? Did you just come from a *funeral?"* and hear her answer, "Yes."

d.d.dawg & Milkbone

You Might Be A WOOFer If:

You spot little ones playing in the park and reminisce about when your *grand*children were that age.

You have to sharpen the hedge trimmers to cut your toenails.

You get a traffic ticket for going 15 miles *under* the speed limit.

You wait 10 minutes in a right turn lane only to discover you're behind a line of parked cars.

You're able to fan yourself with the flap of skin hanging from your upper arm.

You sprinkle crushed TUMS on vanilla ice cream.

You recall your 4th grade boyfriend's name, but can't remember if you took your water pill an hour ago.

You hold a newborn in your arms and have to be reminded where babies come from.

You tell people your age and *no longer* hear, "Oh, you can't be *that* old."

You admit to eating prunes, and *liking* them.

You lie to the hostess seating you at the Early Bird Special Cafe that you're waiting on your aunt.

You order online so the young clerk at your favorite bookstore (whose name you can never remember) won't see you buying books on *memory loss.*

You overhear someone from your graduating class say she was *at least three years behind you.*

Your idea of a "hot time" is eating a hot fudge sundae with extra nuts.

You realize the latest *American Idol* is the same age as your grandson.

You think "bald" is a turn-on.

Your favorite nightshirt says, "Cotton Is Sexy."

You need arm extensions to read the newspaper.

Instead of "Win for Life," you buy lottery tickets with "cash options."

Your granddaughter wants to hear stories about your childhood...because she loves *ancient history.*

There may be no fountain of youth,
But one thing I know is the truth.
If I stay young at heart
The rest of my parts
Will undoubtedly just follow suit.

Mad Dog

List some of the best and worst things about being a WOOFer!

Chapter Eleven

PUPPIES AT HEART

"Age does not protect you from love.
But love, to some extent, protects you from age."
—Jeanne Moreau

"They" say youth is wasted on the young. Thank goodness WOOFers are perpetual puppies at heart.

Puppy Love

I put the moves on my husband the other day. Hooked my finger around his belt loop, and lead him to the den sofa.

Moments into our noon tryst —the one *I'd* instigated—I turned into a sixteen-year-old.

No, I wasn't *really* 16. After all, the fire department's put on standby whenever candles get within 10-feet of my birthday cake. What I mean is, emotionally I regressed to a coy teenager.

Back to that innocent time when curfew was king and a kiss stolen on the couch was daring with parents asleep—

or so we hoped—down the hall.

So there I was, shy as a sophomore, cuddling with my hubby, things ready to bubble when...they unbubbled.

My husband had to board a plane, like he did every Sunday. A weekly ritual I dreaded.

But this day it was with a smile I helped load my husband's suitcase into the van. I joked and laughed. I pinched him in interesting places. I felt young and rejuvenated. No question I'd miss him, but my spirit—and our love—had been markedly recharged and renewed.

Petting, I happily discovered, brings out the *puppy* in an old WOOFer.

d.d.dawg

At the turn of the last century, a woman's life expectancy was only 51 years of age. Heck, nowadays we're just getting started.

The Old Dog
(Who Stayed a Puppy at Heart)

A story about a man may seem out of place in a book for WOOFers, but my life was enhanced by an "old dog" who taught me what it means to age gracefully.

Great Uncle Donald was born in 1897—over 50 years before my birth. He never seemed old to me because he always maintained youthful enthusiasm, joy for life and determination to make the most of every moment.

When I was a kid, he fascinated me with stories about his childhood. Life as an orphan had not been easy, but he cherished the good things from his past and the adversities only made him stronger.

I believe it was that positive outlook on life that allowed him, when the years robbed him of caring for his beloved farm, to find other interests, like becoming an avid reader.

In those golden years, the "old bachelor" (as he often described himself) never stopped appreciating the world around him. Even at 100, his aging eyes still sparkled with childlike wonder at something as beautiful as the full moon shining through his apartment window or as simple as snowflakes gently falling onto the courtyard below him.

My body isn't what it was when I was 25, and whatever I do, I can't stop the aging process. But, if God graces me with the mind to do it, I'll enjoy every minute I have left. And, I'll fight to hold on to as many days as I can. After all, Uncle Donald showed me how to stay a puppy at heart.

Mad Dog

If I Could Turn Back Time

If I could turn back time
I might change a thing or two.
I think I'd study harder
And get more out of school.

Perhaps I wouldn't make
Some choices quite so young;
Or maybe I would finish
Those things I left undone.

I'd prob'ly be more vocal;
And say "I love you" more.
I might take more chances
And open different doors.

But I don't know that I
Would really change that much
For there has been such meaning
In everything I've done.

I learned to treasure joy
Because of tragedy.
I know that I grew stronger
When life was hard for me.

I even found some merit
In each of my mistakes
For every stumble taught me
To just walk on with grace.

Some forks I didn't take
But maybe that was best.
For I found such adventure
On the road ahead.

There's more on my horizon
But if I should die today,
I'm happy with the steps
That brought me all this way.

To have a perfect life
Would not have been for me.
For the journey that I took
Was always meant to be.

Mad Dog

You've Got Male?

Suddenly single in my 50's, I've discovered things are different than they were in my younger dating days. The games are the same, but technology and a more liberal society have changed the way they're played.

Before dating in my *mature* years, I spotted a news story about "tadpoling," which is when an older woman dates a younger man. This method includes math that's way beyond my comprehension. Tadpoling involves taking your age, dividing it in half and then adding seven years to that number. That's supposedly the "perfect" age of the tadpole a "big fish" should try to catch.

"Cougaring," I've been told, is the same thing without the math. You're allowed to aggressively seek men as young as you want. These dating techniques may work for some women, but I can't find the romance in methods that make me picture a big old hound chasing a little puppy.

I've also gotten an education from friends who've used internet dating sites specifically geared towards older women. A picture is apparently not always worth a thousand words. Many potential dates post photos that are a good 15 years old. Translation: "It has been *forever* since I looked like this, but maybe you won't notice if we meet in a dark restaurant."

Then there's the terminology. "Average looking" means an overgrowth of hair everywhere *except* his head. And "physically fit" might mean he can curl empty beer cans. "Huggable" is defined as "I may be older but I'm still a Mama's boy," and "sensitive" says he might cry if you take him to a chick flick.

If the potential relationship involves text messaging, there's a whole new set of abbreviations to learn. "FA" stands for "fat acceptance" (which implies he is), and "BHM" (big handsome man) can be interpreted as "I'm narcissistic." "XXX," on your cell phone screen means something *other* than kisses.

After reviewing these possibilities I've come to the conclusion that for me, there's only one way to approach the world of dating—meet a man in person or through a friend. What could be simpler than sitting face to face and just *talking?*

Mad Dog

Record Time

I sometimes think the world is spinning at 78 rpm, but I'm moving at 33 1/3. Wouldn't it be great to feel 45 rpm again? (And if you don't have the foggiest what 78, 33 1/3 and 45 rpm means, give this book to an over-fifty woman and go listen to your iPod!)

d.d. dawg

What frees your puppy soul?

Chapter Twelve

Over Fifty Tail-Waggers

"One of the keys to happiness is a bad memory."
—Rita Mae Brown

Over 50 Reasons to Wag Our Tails

1. Aging gracefully with a sense of humor.

2. Fearlessly saying, "No."

3. Answering the phone and hearing, "Hi, Grandma!"

4. Qualifying for the senior discount.

5. Stretch capris.

6. Polishing our toenails without the assistance of a chiropractor.

7. Wearing whatever we want.

8. Waking to the smell of fresh coffee.

9. Passing the annual female "plumbing and boob check" with flying colors.

10. Being comfortable going to the movies alone.

11. Opportunities for a new career after retirement.

12. Aqua-aerobics classes to keep the old bones

moving.

13. Good books and popcorn on rainy days.

14. The sound of rain on a tin roof.

15. Having time to volunteer in your local hospital children's ward.

16. Knowing how to e-mail, blog, and Google.

17. The life-lengthening, glorious benefits of chocolate.

18. Even though we're on the downhill run, we're making the most of it.

19. Self-propelled lawn mowers.

20. More time to follow our dreams.

21. A Swedish massage.

22. Self-appreciation regardless of what others may think.

23. Learning to be at peace with our past.

24. Seeing the neighborhood over-run with azaleas in the spring.

25. The joy of giving more than taking.

26. Talking to our children like they're adults and suddenly realizing…they are.

27. Accepting that some dreams never will come true, but that other dreams will take their place.

28. Blubbering through an entire hour of Oprah, guilt-free.

29. Confidence.

30. Accepting that there's a reason for everything whether we understand it or not.

31. With age comes wisdom.

32. Discovering our not-so-flat-anymore tummy is an excellent place to prop books.

33. Those good hair days.

34. Appreciating young ladies and realizing one day they will fill our shoes.

35. Friends who know us better than we know ourselves; who help us like ourselves as much as they like us.

36. Leaving the bed unmade—Mother can't ground us anymore!

37. The chore of rising early is less difficult because we're already awake.

38. Patience comes easier. It's about darn time!

39. Michelle Pfeiffer.

40. Denzel Washington.

41. Lighting candles for someone special—especially ourselves.

42. We can still wag our tails with the best of 'em.

43. Being greeted at the door by our own four-legged tail-wagger.

44. Opening windows on that first sunny, spring day.

45. Hugs.

46. The peace and quiet the first significant snowfall brings—without the chaos of those dreaded school snow days.

47. Having your best friend roar with laughter at a joke that no one in the world but you two would appreciate.

48. The smell of freshly baked bread, and knowing that you baked it.

49. Taking that loaf of bread to a neighbor.

50. Losing the love of your life, and then finding someone who you makes you feel sixteen and alive again!

51. Laughing 'til your stomach hurts.

52. Chocolate.

53. More chocolate.

54. WOOFers.

55. You!

 *List* your *tail-waggers!*

Appendix

WOOFers Club 101

Okay! *Okay!* Sit and stay. We know how WOOFers are (remember, we are three ourselves!), you get a little taste of this **WOOFers Club** stuff and you want more.

So let's get to what it takes to form a **WOOFers Club** chapter.

Visit

www.woofersclub.com

 Step One: Do you know another woman at least 50 years old, and do you believe you can encourage and support each other during this time of life? Yes? Well, there you go. You have a **WOOFers Club.**

 Step Two: Now get together over coffee, lunch or chocolate treat, and convene your charter meeting.

At this gathering, each of you can share and/or select your WOOFer names and breeds.

Choosing a WOOFer name :

When selecting your official WOOFer name, give it considerable thought, as you would naming a new puppy lovingly welcomed into your home. And, remember. The main thing is to make it f-u-n!

Here's how we picked our names:

Diana **"d.d.dawg"** Black fancies herself a Southern Belle, even though she was born and raised a Yankee. Perhaps her nickname, 3D, gives her a multi-dimensional outlook on her heritage, and life in general.

Mary **"Milkbone"** Cunningham's name is a direct reflection of how she sometimes views life. "It's a dog-eat-dog world and I'm wearin' milkbone underwear," she's been heard to growl.

Melinda **"Mad Dog"** Richarz Bailey's WOOF name is a mystery. You couldn't get her riled even if you swiped her favorite chew toy. She doesn't foam at the mouth, and snarling is not in her nature. Maybe she got her name because we're all just *mad* about her.

Determining your WOOFer breed:

Breeding may influence the way a WOOFer reacts to the world around her. After 30 seconds of R&D, the WOOFer Breed Determination Quiz (WBDQ) was developed. WBDQ now makes it possible to verify breed with one simple, but imperative question. Please circle the answer that best describes your reaction to the following scenario. Then look below for a description of your breed.

You enter a party and immediately:

a.   Slink behind the nearest silk ficus

b.   Pounce for the food table

c.   Set off the sprinkler system

d.   Sniff around for the juiciest gossip

e.   Avoid being mistaken for a Vienna sausage

f.   Argue with your shadow

g.   Turn the TV to ESPN

h.   Get hounded

i.   Enter a discussion on dog rights

j.   Look for a pillow and blankie

a. **Bashful Beagle**—You like to stay in the background, preferring to let others take the spotlight. But, one-on-one, your witty sense of humor will leave everyone howling.

b. **Puppy Chow Pooch**—You never meet a dog treat you don't like. You're very sociable and enjoy the company of friends, but don't let them get in the way of "three squares."

c. **Flash Terrier**—You are certainly not a dachshund, but still a "hot dog" in continual *hot flash mode*. You're likely to be found cooling off under the garden hose.

d. **Snobby Schnauzer**—You are a society maven who spends every waking hour organizing charity events and galas. Delegating is impossible because you're the only one who "can do it right."

e. **Half-A-Dog High**—Although you are "vertically challenged," you keep up with the big dogs with your sweet disposition and sparkling personality.

f. **Moody Mutt**—You can change moods with the wind. One minute your tail is wagging and the next you're sinking your teeth into the nearest pants leg.

g. **Springy Spaniel**—You are very athletic. A true sports fanatic, but you're not confined to the sidelines. You're the one running at the head of the pack.

h. **Ravishing Retriever**—You are Westminster "best in show." Perfect clothes, perfect hair, perfect teeth. Old hounds follow you around like puppy dogs.

i. **Bona Fide Fido**—You are confident in your own coat, always self-assured and you never pass up an opportunity to explore the other side of the fence.

j. **Sleep Dog**—You are fond of siestas. You have been known to fall asleep, head first, in your food dish. You prefer lazy, rainy days when you can curl up with a warm afghan.

Here are our WBDQ results:

d.d.dawg's a Bona Fide Fido with a bit (or a LOT) of Puppy Chow Pooch thrown in. She's always rallying for some cause, but not until she's had her breakfast...and lunch...and dinner...oh, and dessert...

Milkbone is a smidgeon of Moody Mutt with a big helping of Puppy Chow Pooch. Don't get between her and a doggy dish!

Mad Dog, never one to sit on the sidelines, is a Springy Spaniel mixed with some Bona Fide Fido and Puppy Chow Pooch. After all, it takes a lot of chow to keep that spring in her dancing paws!

Remember: Register your breed at
www.woofersclub.com
or at
www.woofersclub.blogspot.com

Step Three*:* To ensure a strong sisterhood, during each meeting, repeat the WOOFers Pledge:

WOOFers, WOOFers, WOOFers are we.
Women Only Over Fifty.
We are in a real dogfight
With hormones and our appetites.
But, we know we will prevail
Between our legs, no tucked in tail!
We may be larger than size three
But we're still proud as we can be.
No sleeping dogs—we do not lie
Cause we bark at this phase of life.
Each day we struggle up the hill
Wagging on with steadfast will.
We know we will come out on top
Despite quite frequent hydrant stops.
Over the hill, some might say
But every dog has her day.
So we growl, "Grow old with me—
Top dogs, the best is yet to be!"
WOOFers, WOOFers, WOOFers are we.
Women Only Over Fifty!

🐾 ***Step Four****:* Now howl together in celebration of **WOOF** by singing the official anthem. (It's more or less sung to the tune of "If You're Happy and You Know It Clap Your Hands.")

Oh, we're proud to be WOOFers
Yes indeed (Yes, indeed)
Oh we're proud to be WOOFers
Yes indeed (Yes, indeed!)
Yes, we're proud to be WOOFers
(We ain't no *pussyfooters*!)
Oh, we're proud to be WOOFers
Yes indeed (Yes indeed!)

And that's it! What could be easier than starting a chapter of **WOOFers Club?**

(Your official WOOFers Club name)

Women Only Over Fifty
with a new leash on life!

REMEMBER THIS, ABOVE ALL ELSE...

"FIFTY IS NOT

THE END...

IT'S ONLY THE BEGINNING!"

About the Authors

Diana Black, a graduate of Indiana University, combines her love of words and the visual arts to create everything from children's stories and freelance articles to Web designs and book illustrations.

A certified grant professional and published songwriter, author, and cartoonist, she has a daughter and granddaughter, and lives with her husband near the quaint, historic town square of Marietta, Georgia.

www.diana-designs.net
www.thebeetgoesonblog.blogspot.com

Mary Cunningham makes her home in the beautiful mountains of West Georgia with her husband and adopted woofie, Molly. Parents of three children, they are also blessed with a fifteen-year-old granddaughter.

In addition to WOOF, she is the author of the tween fantasy series, *Cynthia's Attic*, and a member of SCBWI (Southern Breeze Chapter), The Georgia Reading Association and the Carrollton Creative Writers Club.

www.marycunninghambooks.com
www.cynthiasattic.blogspot.com

Melinda Richarz Bailey earned a B.A. in Journalism from the University of North Texas. A free lance writer for over 40 years, she has authored several books and articles published in *True West*, *Kids, Etc.*, *Reminisce*, *Cats Magazine*, *Frontier Times*, *Nashville Parent*, and *Cincinnati Family Magazine*.

The co-recipient of the Academy of Western Artists 2004 Will Rogers Award for Song of the Year, she currently resides in Tyler, Texas.

Printed in the United States
121334LV00001B/172-288/P

9 781590 806067